Little Whiskers
of Wisdom

© 2009 by Barbour Publishing, Inc.

Compiled by Katherine Douglas.

ISBN 978-1-60260-467-4

Published by Barbour Publishing, Inc., P.O. Box 719, Uhrichsville, Ohio 44683, www.barbourbooks.com.

Our mission is to publish and distribute inspirational products offering exceptional value and biblical encouragement to the masses.

Printed in the United States of America.

LITTLE WHISKERS
OF WISDOM

BARBOUR
PUBLISHING

Cats start their day with a satisfied stretch and a long drink of water. Not a half-bad idea for starting your day today!

A cat will never drown if she sees the shore.

Francis Bacon

We won't drown in our own sea of troubles
if we keep focused on eternity's shore.

There's something about the presence
of a cat. . .that takes the bite
out of being alone.

Louis Camuti

There is no more intrepid
explorer than a kitten.

JULES CHAMPFLEURY

Kittens play with one another in reckless abandon. Try laughing and loving today with reckless abandon, and watch the results spread to those around you. A tumble in playfulness can upend a tension-filled situation.

"Scaredy cat" describes the high-strung feline response when caught off guard. But cats quickly return to their usual calm with little more than a pat on the head. What calms you? A whispered praise to God? A pat on the back? Open yourself up to unlikely sources of serenity.

Cats love to extend their claws and enjoy a place in the sun. Find your own spot in the sunshine. Simple things that cost nothing can bring moments of refreshing peace.

Nobody likes to clean the litter box.
Be courteous. Pick up after yourself.
Then go the extra mile:
Clean the litter box.

A famous portrait shows a young girl in traditional mourning attire. She clutches a snow-white cat to her chest. When things are bleakest, sometimes all we can do is hold on to our whiskered friends.

Just like us, the condition of a cat's fur or skin is indicative of what she's eating and how she's handling stress. If both you and your cat are losing hair, it may be time to change diets, de-stress, or find a new groomer.

When the cat's away, the mice will play. Does *our* play take into account that "the eyes of the Lord range throughout the earth" (2 Chronicles 16:9 NIV)?

There are two means of refuge from the miseries of life: music and cats.

ALBERT SCHWEITZER

Cats like to dig their claws into a scratching post for a good workout. Likewise, it may be time for us to put on the running shoes or tone up with some aerobic exercise.

Even when a tornado strikes or the flood waters come, cats have little problem holding their own when they're alone. They're self-sufficient and independent. Sometimes we have to lift our chin, square our shoulders, and weather life's storms one thunderclap at a time.

Dogs have owners; cats have staff.
If you want to be in charge,
don't get a cat.

Stealth and sneakiness—the barn cat's *modus operandi*. A pampered house cat needs no such character qualities. Neither do we—unless we're in espionage.

Newborn kittens mew and whimper constantly. Sometimes we have family members who continually whine because of ill health or loneliness. Can we exercise the same patience with them as the newborn kittens' mother does with her brood?

We barely get the litter box cleaned and shoveled out, and the cat's back in it. In a nanosecond, our favorite feline is messing up what we just cleaned.
Christ alone can clean up and shovel out the messes we make in the litter boxes of our lives.

No matter how much cats fight,
there always seems to
be plenty of kittens.

ABRAHAM LINCOLN

One of the most striking differences
between a cat and a lie is that
a cat has only nine lives.

MARK TWAIN

Cats are rather delicate creatures. . .subject to a good many ailments, but I never heard of one who suffered from insomnia.

JOSEPH WOOD KRUTCH

Having his belly rubbed tells a cat he's noticed and cared for. A small smile, a genuine greeting, or a firm handshake may be all it takes to tell someone, "I see you. You are important."

Cats mew, meow, and howl. What they
do the most tells us a lot about them.
People complain, criticize, and encourage.
What we do the most tells a lot about us, too.
How does your cat—or others—hear you today?

Peoplе that don't likе cats
havеn't mеt thе right onе yеt.

DEBORAH A. EDWARDS

Most children love kittens. Unfortunately, some children have terrible allergies to cats. Denying ourselves or someone else a good thing isn't easy or fun. But sometimes it's necessary.

Some cats have an uncanny sense of danger. They warn us with upstanding fur, dilated pupils, or erratic behavior. Their inherent warning systems have been known to alert their owners to smoldering fires or suspicious visitors. Be glad for your cat's innate warning system.

Cartoon cats may be heroes or villains.
Some, like Jim Davis's Garfield, are pranksters.
What does your nominee for Favorite
Famous Cat say about you?

Cats like to eat fish, but they're not willing to get wet to catch one. Are you willing to get wet—or work hard—for what you really want?

Cats don't like to take medicine no matter how well we dress it up, cover it up, or smash it up. When we're getting the medicine we deserve (or need), do we act like our cats? Or do we submit and take it without making the fur fly?

Some cats enjoy listening to classical music.
They settle in, relax, and surround themselves with
the beauty of Verdi or Beethoven. Turn up the music.
Surround yourself with some beautiful melodies.
Give way to some minutes of relaxation
and auditory bliss.

There are no ordinary cats.

Sidonie Gabrielle

Cats seem to go on the principle that it never does any harm to ask for what you want.

JOSEPH WOOD KRUTCH

After scolding one's cat, one looks into its face and
is seized by the ugly suspicion that it understood
every word. And has filed it for reference.

CHARLOTTE GRAY

Cats mark what's theirs when they affectionately rub their whiskered faces against our legs. An affectionate touch often speaks louder than words.

The godly care for their animals.

PROVERBS 12:10 NLT

Little things matter to God.
How we do our jobs. How we manage
money. How we treat our cats.

Dogs come when they're called; cats take a message and get back to you later.

MARY BLY

Show cats get poofed up and spruced up to look their best for the judges. When we want to make a good impression, it doesn't hurt to take a look in the mirror first.

If a dog jumps in your lap, it is because he is fond of you; but if a cat does the same thing, it is because your lap is warmer.

ALFRED NORTH WHITEHEAD

Women and cats will do as they please,
and men and dogs should relax
and get used to the idea.

ROBERT A. HEINLEIN

Cats eat almost anything. Bugs. Grass. Butterflies. Cat food. Unsuspecting goldfish. Yet they're very selective about those with whom they socialize. For health reasons, we have to be selective about our food. For moral reasons, we have to be selective about our choice of friends.

We can handle domestic cats. Bobcats, tigers, and leopards aren't so easily managed. Sometimes we can resist temptation with wisdom and resolve. Sometimes it's best to run.

Picture kittens and children together.
Don't you feel better already?

When two aircraft do battle aloft, it's called a dogfight. When two women come to blows, it's called a catfight. Just goes to show: Not everything in life can be readily understood or explained.

When company comes, pesky cats often find themselves confined to one room. Not infrequently, the pests will thump impatiently at the door to be heard, if not seen. Our heavenly Father doesn't confine us to our room when we're pesky. No need to thump at His door for attention!

The smallest feline is a masterpiece.

LEONARDO DA VINCI

Tangled fur is no fun for cats or their owners.
Neither are the tangled webs
we weave of our lives.

Kittens are such a nice way
to start cats.

Because of their unique grooming practices, cats cough up hair balls. When was the last time you were thankful for simple things like hairbrushes and combs?

A little drowsy cat is an image
of perfect beatitude.

JULES CHAMPFLEURY

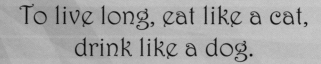

To live long, eat like a cat,
drink like a dog.

GERMAN PROVERB

Two cats in the Disney classic *Lady and the Tramp* sing that, whether we're pleased about it or not, they're Siamese cats. All of us are wise to remember that, whether or not it pleases us, we've been made in God's image.

Cats love the pungent smell of catnip.
Lived well, our lives can be
a sweet aroma to others.

Catty. Cat-o'-nine-tails. Cat's paw.
All bad things that cats have had nothing to
do with. We may get blamed for things
we had nothing to do with either.
We just need to move on.

Cats in Burkina Faso, Africa, don't "pussyfoot around" when it comes to green mamba snakes. They double as family pets and protectors from venomous snakes.

Cats have suffered the extremes of worship and mistreatment. Sadly enough, they've received both at the hands of people. People have not been the better for either extreme.

Cats are persistent hunters and shameless loungers: good role models when we work on a project until its completion.

Our cats comfort and entertain us. They soothe us with their purring and crack us up with their antics. Maybe it's time to share our cat with the widow next door, or the latchkey kid across the street. Why not invite someone in for cocoa and cat watching?

According to the Humane Society of the United States, one female cat and her offspring can produce about 420,000 cats in seven years. "Moderation in all things" holds true in almost every instance.

There's not much that's as pleasing to the eye as a little girl gently cradling a kitten.

Your cat will never threaten your popularity by barking at three in the morning. He won't attack the mailman or the drapes, although he may climb the drapes to see how the room looks from the ceiling.

HELEN POWERS

Mother cats: nurturing and patient.
Feral cats: unpredictable and skittish.
Which cat category might we fit into?

If cats could talk, they wouldn't.

NAN PORTER

If you're struggling to make new friends after a long-distance move, you might try getting a kitten. If no one ventures to make your acquaintance, you've still gained one new friend.

Cats always know whether people like or dislike them. They do not always care enough to do anything about it.

WINIFRED CARRIERE

When we're tempted to pass along some gossip, it's best to recall the words of Will Rogers: "Lettin' the cat outta the bag is a whole lot easier 'n puttin' it back in."

Cat people are different, to the extent that they generally are not conformists. How could they be, with a cat running their lives?

LOUIS CAMUTI

The Bible's only references to cats are to big cats. Like this one: "Watch out for your great enemy, the devil. He prowls around like a roaring lion, looking for someone to devour. Stand firm against him, and be strong in your faith" (1 Peter 5:8-9 NLT).

Beware of people who dislike cats.

IRISH PROVERB

Who among us hasn't envied a cat's
ability to ignore the cares of daily life
and to relax completely?

KAREN BRADENMEYER

On average, cats sleep between sixteen
and eighteen hours a day.

The hour has come for you to wake
from sleep. For salvation is nearer to us
now than when we first believed.

ROMANS 13:11 ESV

As every cat owner knows,
nobody owns a cat.

ELLEN PERRY BERKELEY

Having one of those days when you feel
like you've been trying to herd cats?
Some tasks can't be done. Know when to say
"enough." Then tackle the next project.

A cat has absolute emotional honesty:
Human beings, for one reason or another,
may hide their feelings, but a cat does not.

Ernest Hemingway

A cat will be your friend,
but never your slave.

THEOPHILE GAUTIER

A cat will write her autograph
all over your leg if you let her.

MARK TWAIN

Through good times and bad,
whether we want them or not,
God's fingerprints are all over us.

Cats carefully calculate the distance, dig in, and spring with determined precision. They can perform astounding leaps. You might surprise yourself with what you can do when you put your mind to it.

In the Middle Ages, cats were almost brought to extinction for being "of the devil," and the plague-carrying rat population decimated Europe as a result. Superstition breeds havoc when taken seriously.

In ancient times cats were worshipped
as gods; they have not forgotten this.

TERRY PRATCHETT

A healthy cat is more likely to be better behaved and happy. So are healthy people.

Cats have been known to climb—and knock down—Christmas trees. Toddlers have pulled down their share of Christmas trees, too. Neither makes for a very merry Christmas. But both make for a great story later. *Much later.*

A cat pours his body on the floor like water. It is restful just to see him.

WILLIAM LYON PHELPS

People have had cats that left for days, weeks, or even months. Then one day, the cat suddenly returns without explanation. Their owners are glad to have them back. If we can show the same welcoming grace to wandering children, we may gain them back for (their) good, too.

Some say it's a dog-eat-dog world.
Makes you glad you live with a cat.

To err is human, to purr is feline.

Robert Byrne

Cats do not like fleas, ticks, or ear mites.
Like things that irritate or hurt us, they're all facts of
life. We can't expect life to be irritant—or flea—free.

Cats vomit hair balls, food, and ingested items that should not have been eaten in the first place. Cats aren't the only ones who make messes that require someone else to clean up after them.

Cats cry pitifully when they're exhausted and trapped.
So do some of us. But we have hope.

The eyes of the LORD are on the righteous
and his ears are attentive to their cry.

PSALM 34:15 NIV

Sometimes cats get switched because they look so much alike. If you're a "multiple," be glad God gave parents the ability to tell their look-alikes apart.

It always gives me a shiver when I see
a cat seeing what I can't see.

ELEANOR FARJEON

A dozen cats were brought in to (successfully) save the inventory of a biscuit factory in England. Before that, mouse traps and rat poison failed. Hired hunting dogs ate more biscuits than mice. Lesson: Don't send a dog for a job only a cat can do.

If there's one spot of sun spilling onto the floor, a cat will find it and soak it up.

J. A. McIntosh

If you are allergic to a thing, it is best
not to put that thing in your mouth,
particularly if the thing is cats.

LEMONY SNICKET

Well-fed cats make the best mousers.
Likewise, children, coworkers, and friends whose
"diets" are supplemented with appreciation for the
little things they do will excel at bigger things.

A member of a rock 'n' roll band once had a cat that would sleep inside the bass drum while the band practiced. Some cats, like some teenagers, find solace in head-banging music.

By and large, people who enjoy teaching animals to roll over will find themselves happier with a dog.

BARBARA HOLLAND

Cats are connoisseurs of comfort.

JAMES HERRIOT

The cat is the only animal which
accepts the comforts but rejects
the bondage of domesticity.

GEORGES LOUIS LECLERC DE BUFFON

To keep a true perspective of one's importance, everyone should have a dog that will worship him and a cat that will ignore him.

DEREKE BRUCE

I had been told that the training procedure with cats was difficult. It's not. Mine had me trained in two days.

BILL DANA

Wise cat owners don't allow their pets to have dangerous toys. Just as we keep some things from our cats or our children, God keeps some things from us—no matter how much we badger Him for them.

An Arab proverb says a cat once bitten by a snake dreads even rope. In the same way, neighbors who have been bitten by our sharp words won't remain our friends.

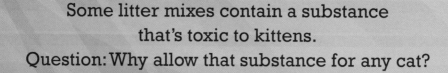

Some litter mixes contain a substance
that's toxic to kittens.
Question: Why allow that substance for any cat?

We have a rating system for movies
in the United States.
Question: If a movie isn't suitable for children,
is it suitable for adults?

Comic-strip character Garfield the cat has a household companion, Odie the dog. Just like siblings, they torment each other, play jokes on one another, and battle for attention. Enjoy the entertainment—even the small frustrations—of having children around the house. They'll be gone before you know it.

The ideal of calm exists in a sitting cat.

JULES REYNARD

Some cats won't eat certain types of food in one particular room of a house, but they'll eat it in another. Makes you wonder if your finicky toddler has been studying the family cat.

Here's a secret: Foods that are labeled "lite" usually make cats want to eat more. (Aha! Maybe that's why we continue to pack on the pounds even though we eat "lite" foods.)

If we treated everyone we met with the same affection we bestow upon our favorite cat, they, too, would purr.

MARTIN BUXBAUM

A cat expert says that handling a cat in the wrong way or at the wrong time can get the handler hurt. Even if we're careful in our "handling" of others, we may still get hurt. Like cats, people need some time alone, too.

When cats are frightened, they lose hair quickly. When another animal grabs him, the cat's fur comes out easily. Result? The predator loses his grip. Resolve to shed bad habits that hold you in their grip.

After the Scottish sailor Alexander Selkirk was
shipwrecked and marooned off the coast of Chile
in the early 1700s, he credited the friendship
of island cats and parrots for his sanity
during his four years of isolation.

With dogs and people, it's love in big splashy colors. . . . With a cat, you're dealing in pastels.

LOUIS CAMUTI

Cats, like people, don't like change. If you're contemplating a move, you and your cat can help each other through the transition.

Cat owners must be diligent to protect their cats from itchy ear mites. We must avoid "having itching ears" (2 Timothy 4:3 KJV), too, taking care that we don't turn away our ears from the truth.

Cats will walk in the direction of whatever it is they want. How many of us "beat around the bush" when we want something? Try simple straightforwardness.

Cats almost always make perfect landings,
no matter the height from which they jump or tumble.
The same can't be said for us. Even if we've covered
every contingency, we make errors in judgment.
Work on your next project with wisdom born of humility.

Cats are like people. When we get old, everything we do is more of a challenge.

ANNIE BRUCE

Sometimes cats get themselves into tight spots from which they can't extricate themselves without aid. They meow for help. We get ourselves into tight spots, too. We may have to swallow our pride and "meow" for help, also.

As cats get older, they often mellow to their canine counterparts. In fact, they may find that "lying down with dogs" affords them some extra body heat when it's cold. Don't wait for bad circumstances to force you to befriend others unlike yourself.

Cats aren't partial to people
who are wealthy and famous.
What's inside a person captures
their attention and affection.

The smart cat doesn't let on that he is.

H. G. FROMMER

Cats know the difference between cat food and cat litter. Do we recognize the difference when it comes to entertainment that's fit for "consumption"?

Fact: When a kitten isn't handled much or at all,
he may grow up to dislike handling or holding.
Touch and hold your kittens—
and your children—often.

Even overweight cats instinctively know the cardinal rule: When fat, arrange yourself in slim poses.

JOHN WEITZ

There is no snooze button on
a cat who wants breakfast.

UNKNOWN

If purring could be encapsulated, it would
be the most powerful antidepressant
in the pharmaceutical market.

ALEXIS F. HOPE

Kittens are born with their eyes shut.
They open them in about six days, take a
look around, then close them again
for the better part of their lives.

STEPHEN BAKER

The domestic cat is a modern-day success story. Small, clean, self-sufficient, and self-assured. . .

BRUCE FOGLE

Just as there are latchkey children, there are latchkey cats. Despite occasional feline fights and bad weather, latchkey cats probably fare somewhat better than their human counterparts.

Don't call the fire department.
Given enough time, hunger pangs, and lack of
an audience, any cat stuck in a tree will come
down. Sometimes all that's needed to get out
of a bad situation is time alone to think.

Cats don't hunt flies and eat them in hopes of a satisfying meal. Hunting for flies sharpens the cat's stealth and agility.

Cats' whiskers are as long as the widest part of their bodies. So equipped, they can tell whether or not to proceed through a tight spot. Carefully praying through a possible course of action, the Bible, and wise friends offer us the same protection.

One cat owner says that walking and fresh air help relieve stress. She was writing about cats. She could just as easily have been writing about people. Ready for a walk?

The cat is mighty dignified
until the dog comes by.

AMERICAN PROVERB

An occasional snack of grass benefits the feline diet. An occasional snack of dark chocolate benefits the human diet. Ah, such bliss in life's little blessings.

When a cat arches her back, flattens out her ears, and hisses, she's warning others not to mess with her. A wise person, like a smart cat owner, picks up on obvious—or cloaked—signals. And they know when to maintain a safe distance.

Abyssinian cats tend to be quiet while Siamese cats are quite vocal. Persian cats loathe teasing, whereas Rex cats enjoy playing games. We need to show people the same understanding for their peculiarities that we so easily acknowledge in cats.

Purring would seem to be. . .an automatic safety valve device for dealing with happiness overflow.

DEBBIE PETERSON

One veterinarian says that people all over the world recognize both themselves and their cats in the character of Jim Davis's Garfield, making the whiskered whiner all the more lovable. If that's true, Garfield has to be the world's only beloved whiner.

A lame cat is better than a swift horse when rats infest the palace.

CHINESE PROVERB

Some have said their cats would rather be petted than eat. Love-starved people are not unlike those felines. They devour any attentiveness or interest because of a hidden hunger. All of us, sooner or later, experience those kinds of hunger pangs.

I care not much for a man's religion
whose dog and cat are not better for it.

ABRAHAM LINCOLN

Anyone who sets himself up as "religious" by talking a good game is self-deceived. This kind of religion is hot air. . . . Real religion. . .is this: Reach out to the homeless and loveless in their plight, and guard against corruption from the godless world.

JAMES 1:26–27 MSG

Canadian Sphynx cats are known for their hairlessness. They do technically have hair—it's just very short and more like peach fuzz than fur. Even with cats, appearances can be deceiving.

Geneticists plan to breed "hypoallergenic cats" so that people with cat allergies can have cats. Few, however, are asking what such gene manipulation will do to the cat. Just because we can do something, should we?

Cats are as varied as people.
Their eyes, their bodies, their habits,
their strengths, their weaknesses.
Variety surrounds us! Enjoy it.

Meow is like *aloha*.
It can mean anything.

HANK KETCHUM

Russian clown Yuri Kuklachev performs regularly with his trained cats. The secret of his success, he says, comes from knowing no one can force a cat to do anything.

According to one feline expert, Abyssinian cats are opinionated, attention-seeking athletes. Unlike many professional athletes, Abyssinians are the only ones that can show such character traits and still be likeable.

It's really the cat's house—
we just pay the mortgage.

UNKNOWN

A cat is a lion in a jungle
of small bushes.

INDIAN PROVERB

James Herriot said when he began his veterinary practice that he was afraid he'd never get to work with his favorite animal, the cat. Yet everywhere he went on farms throughout the North Yorkshire Dales, cats were there. Expect to find small delights in unlikely places.

Longhaired cats may flaunt their hirsute handsomeness; in purely coat terms, it is svelte shorthairs who generally have the upper paw.

BRUCE FOGLE

Every life should have nine cats.

ANONYMOUS

Whiskers are an important part of a cat's sensory detection. They're not unlike those eyes mothers have in the backs of their heads. And just as important.

Cats frequently clean their coats with their tongues. Occasionally, they will develop hair balls that have to be surgically removed.

Fact: Cats respond most readily to names that end in a long-E sound. Fact: People respond most readily to requests that end in "please."

The cat is domestic only as far as it suits its own ends.

SAKI

Most cats want what they want when they want it—which is now. Even felines have learned that "the squeaky wheel gets the grease."

An old proverb says that those who play with cats must expect to be scratched. Risks abound in every undertaking. Take a risk. Try something new today!

Pet psychologist John Wright says that if we treat a cat like it's dangerous and evil, it's not likely to become social or friendly. It's best to give people and pets the benefit of the doubt. One may reward us with a smile, the other with a purr.

The cat could very well be man's best friend,
but would never stoop to admitting it.

Doug Larson

Never give anyone reason to be
embarrassed to call you "friend."

American Bobtail cats speak
in soft chirps and trills.

A soft answer turns away wrath.

PROVERBS 15:1 ESV

As cats age, their eyesight deteriorates, their hair often thins in different places, and their joints ache. As we age, we have an empathetic soul mate in our aging cats.

There's a breed of cat called "Munchkins." Sometimes they're called "rug huggers." Name-calling often says more about us than the pet or the person we've labeled with an unflattering nickname.

Who would believe such pleasure
from a wee ball o' fur?

IRISH PROVERB

[My cat] clawed her way into
my heart and wouldn't let go.

MISSY ALTIJD

When a cat's tail swishes back and forth, it doesn't automatically mean he's angry. Cats wag their tails when they're conflicted. One wonders if that's why two-year-old children "wag" their heads so often.

Cats roll over onto their backs to show trust.
They make themselves vulnerable to us.
When other people make themselves vulnerable
to us, do we protect their secrets?
Do we show them that we can be trusted?

All Children Left Unattended Will Be Given a Free Kitten.

Sign in a veterinarian's office

I'm not much of a cook. My favorite thing to make from scratch is a purr.

UNKNOWN

To escort a cat on a leash is against the nature of a cat. It is the nature of cats to do a certain amount of unescorted roaming.

ADLAI STEVENSON

Siamese cats have been called chatterboxes who thrive on attention. They enjoy the companionship of other cats or people. Are you a people person among few other people persons? A Siamese cat might be a fine companion to share your lonely evenings.

Cats have an infallible understanding of total concentration—and get between you and it.

ARTHUR BRIDGES

There was an old bulldog named Caesar,
Who went for a cat just to tease her;
But she spat and she spit,
Till the old bulldog quit.
Now when poor Caesar sees her, he flees her.

UNKNOWN

At eighteen years of age a cat is about eighty-seven
years old in people years. How refreshing to have
a "teenager" about the house when it's a feline.
If you're up in years and your cat is, too,
you're a good match for each other!

Ever feel as "nervous as a cat in a room full of rocking chairs"? Picture that scene— and you'll find yourself smiling.

According to cat experts, purring doesn't always mean contentment. Purring may signal pain, fear, or be a cry for help.

Even in laughter the heart may ache.

PROVERBS 14:13 ESV

Cats stiffen up their legs and arch their backs to appear bigger and scarier to a foe. Are we ever guilty of posing— of putting on a false front?

Cats are the natural companions of intellectuals. They are silent watchers of dreams, inspiration, and patient research.

Dr. Fernand Mery

If your children are rowdy or someone in the house is grumpy, try some music therapy. The lilting notes of Frank Bjorn's 1962 piano classic, "Alley Cat," might brighten the whole house after just a few bars.

Cats know the best spots for sleeping and bird watching. Follow your cat today. Expect to find a good place for some relaxation.

Sylvester and Tweety Bird, classic cartoon characters dating from 1947, enjoyed a love/hate relationship. Some of us find ourselves in difficult familial relationships similar to that of Tweety and Sylvester. When change isn't likely to come any time soon, whisper the "Serenity Prayer," and hold on to hope.

An old adage says a cat in gloves catches no mice. There are hard things in life we can't handle with kid gloves. Sometimes situations call for a firm hand. It may be with misbehaving children. It may be in the practice of our own self-control.

Cats are such agreeable friends; they ask no
questions, they pass no criticisms.

George Eliot

Cats are poetry in motion.
Dogs are gibberish in neutral.

UNKNOWN

Books and cats and fair-haired little girls
make the best furnishings for a room.

FRENCH PROVERB

So the LORD God formed from the ground all the wild animals and all the birds of the sky. He brought them to the man to see what he would call them, and the man chose a name for each one.

GENESIS 2:19 NLT